Peacock

Amazing Animal Books for Young Readers

By
K. Bennett

Mendon Cottage Books

JD-Biz Publishing

Read More Amazing Animal Books

Purchase at Amazon.com

Table of Contents

Introduction

Chapter 1 Fascinating Peacocks

Chapter 2 Peacock's Features

Chapter 3 A Peacock's Life

Conclusion Fun Peacock Facts!

Author Bio

Introduction

Peacocks are a magnificent species from the Pheasant family of birds. The ***Pavo Cristatus*** or Indian Peafowl is a large bird. It is well-known for their beautiful, bright tails in dazzling colors and hues! Have you ever seen one?

The Pheasant family of birds includes partridges, chickens, jungle fowls, quails and of course the peafowl. This species comes from South Asia and today, Peacocks are found in places like Sri Lanka, Bangladesh, Pakistan, Western China and India among others.

Another variation of the bird is found in Burma and in the lush African Rainforests, the Congo Peacock is happy living under the stars. Sadly, this species has not been seen for years, but it just may pop up one day again!

Did you know only males are actually Peacocks? So what are females called? The female species of this bird is a Peahen and when both (or a group) are together they are known as: Peafowls. And the babies? They are known as Peachicks! Life expectancy is usually between 15 – 20 years. But there is a record of a bird living in captivity for 23 years.

It is interesting to note that in this species the male really dazzles, but the female is more subdued. How so? Males are the ones with the bright plumage and long impressive train or tail. Some females have no train and although their neck area has beautiful greenish feathers, their plumage is mostly a dull brown.

Peacocks live off the ground. They are known as "ground feeders" according to *National Geographic*. This means their food is found— you guessed it— on the ground! They eat things like berries, grains, insects and even small animals like lizards, rodents (Small) and snakes.

For thousands of years Peacocks have been admired for their plumage and personality. Have you ever heard of the term 'Proud as a Peacock?' A writer who lived many years ago used this phrase (Written as *Proud a Pekok – by Chaucer in Troilus & Criseyde*) to describe personality traits. This term stuck in everyone's mind and when we use this phrase, we may think of a proud or ostentatious person.

There is no doubt Peacocks are unique and distinctive. But in some places they are more than just a bird. Did you know this bird is sacred to many people especially in India? In the Hindu religion this beautiful bird is revered for its tail, which symbolizes the 'eyes of the gods.'

Ultimately, Peacocks are amazing birds and a beautiful part of nature's wonders!

Chapter 1

As previously mentioned, Peacocks are one of nature's most distinctive birds. There are two Asiatic species known as the Indian Peafowl and the Green Peafowl. There is also an African species known as the Congo Peacock. Each one of these birds has unique color markings to tell them apart.

The discovery of the African species is quite an interesting story. In 1913, a single feather of this bird was found and a search began to locate the mysterious owner. It took many years but finally in 1936, the *Afropavo Congensis* —the Congo Peacock— was discovered!

Beautiful colors

A tail by any other

The male peacock has an impressive train or tail. Usually during its 5th to 6th year, the male's tail is the brightest and most beautiful. This train is approximately 60 percent of the Peacock's body length. When mating season approaches, the Peacock uses its ornamental tail for all its worth. The male arches his feathers and extends them like a dazzling multicolored fan. It's like he's saying to the female: *Hey. It's me…please say hello!*

The tail of the Peacock has an amazing design. The 'eyes' of the tail are known as the ***Ocelli*** or eye spots. The male uses this design to attract as many females as he can. But these designs are not just for beauty. They actually complete a function. How so?

The Oxford Journals on Behavioral Ecology studied this process and noted something interesting. When the male extends his feathers he angles it against the light of the sun. Depending on the degree of the angle, the male will attract lots of females. However, if the angle is wrong the mating success will be low. Quite an intriguing factor to consider, don't you think?

 ### *One of the largest birds*

We already know how much percentage of the tail is part of a Peacocks body. But we have not discussed wingspan or the length of the wings. These birds are large and they can fly. However, for the most part, they stay on the ground until flight is necessary.

National Geographic measures their body size as 35 – 50 inches and the tail at approximately 5 – 6 feet. They can weigh between 8.75 to 13 pounds and wingspan is approximately 4.5 – 5.2 feet.

Next to a full grown person Peacocks are quite large!

What do they eat?

As noted in the introduction, Peacocks are ground feeders and their diet is quite varied. They are omnivores so they eat things like insects, berries, wild figs and reptiles. Some Peacocks are pets and others are in zoos. They love black sunflower seeds, fruit, bread and even table scraps. Some of them also forage for other tidbits to eat. This could include spiders and amphibious creatures. The truth is if they like it, they will eat it!

Chapter 2

Peacocks like all other creatures have distinct personality traits. The Green peafowl is more aggressive by nature and not necessarily mild, so if they are kept in captivity they need to remain apart. They don't like the cold either.

In contrast, the Indian Peafowl is more of a domestic creature and mild-tempered. They don't mind the cold like the Green Peacocks, and can survive Northern winters if necessary. In captivity, these birds will allow you to get close and even hand feed them. But touching them is another matter!

Indian Peafowls can also get very upset when unexpected events invade their territory. For example, if there are loud noises or pets running around including small kids, the 'Indian Blues' may begin to pant or heave in clear signs of distress. Other than this, the Indian Peafowls are beautiful birds and relatively easy to handle.

This is my best side!

The African Peafowl species (Exclusive to the dense rainforests of the Congo) is a very special bird. Unlike the other two species the male helps the female to protect and feed the baby peachicks. Quite a responsible father, don't you think?

Habitat

In the wild, Peacocks prefer certain living arrangements to make them happy. Their preference is somewhere along the following list:

- Nest on the ground but roost in the trees
- Forest areas
-Orchards
-Stream-side forests
-Cultivated land.

Birdsflight.com notes Peacocks living arrangements extend to maple and pine trees, oaks and cedars.

Predators

Peacocks have a very distinctive cry, and can produce up to 11 vocalizations or sounds. Some people say this call is ugly. Do you know why? The reason has to do with the sound of the call. Some people say it sounds like someone crying for help!

Have you ever heard a Peacock's cry? Ask your parents or a guardian to help you search online.

However, many creatures appreciate the Peacocks loud cry. Why? Well, if a predator is around who is the first bird to sound the warning? The one who lets everyone know danger is near? Yes! The Peacock is your bird of call. Their loud cry will sound the warning and help everyone get away safe.

Peacocks have to keep a good watch. Wild dogs, tigers, leopards and even raccoons are a constant danger. Safety in numbers keeps many of these birds safe from predators. But the males are not the only ones who keep watch. A female will cry out to warn other females of danger.

You may think a Peacock can't hide very well. After all, they have such a long tail everyone can see it for miles! And yet, this species has developed magnificent adaptation skills. Remember the Peacocks tail?

If a predator gets near, the bird waits for the right moment and then whoosh! Out comes the tail and the predator freezes like a deer in the headlights. Soon they are off and running and the Peacock escapes safely. This does not work with all predators, but it does help in some cases.

This cycle of life is one reason why Peacocks like to roost high in trees with lots of big leaves. If it is a good sleeping spot, the Peacock may return there for many nights. It not only gives them peace of mind but a good night's sleep!

White Peacocks

You probably think White Peafowls are Albinos, but this is not the case. Why? Albinos have an absence of pigmentation, but White Peafowls have beautiful blue eyes. And when the little chicks are small they are yellow! As they get older and mature, they turn into a magnificent display of White feathers. *Tonyhill.net* calls them: *"a color variation of the India Blue Peacock."* As you may guess, these birds are rare and hard to find!

FUN FACTS FOR KIDS: Many years ago, medieval Knights made a promise called the *"Vow of the Peacock."* To celebrate this vow, knights would decorate their helmet with the beautiful feathers of the Peacock. Do you know what this *Vow of the Peacock* is? Ask your parents or a guardian to help you research this topic. To give you a head start, research the writings of Charles Dickens from the Victorian Periodical entitled: *All Year Round.* Have fun!

Daily life

Peacocks have an established daily routine. We have already talked about their night rest in the trees. But during the day they wander around on the ground. It is customary for them to divide into smaller groups and wander around their habitat.

Some forage for food and others preen their feathers. Some rest in the shade and spend a nice restful day. This behavior is typical during the warmer hours especially at noon. During the evening hours they continue to forage for food, may have some water to drink and then it's time to rest.

During the mating season this behavior changes. There may groups of females or groups of males or even groups of females with one male.

Look over here!

Anything for a show

When a male is out for a walk or stroll, his tail lies over his back and trails behind him. But if a female is near and he feels like 'showing off' then whoosh! Like a radiant fan, he will arch his tail and angle it against the sunlight. If the female seems interested the male gets even more creative. He will shimmer or flash his colors to catch her eye. Whatever it takes to be seen is pretty much what he will do!

Brilliant display

Early beginnings

A Peahen matures in a couple years and then she lays eggs. And these eggs are about 3 times the size of chicken eggs. Sometimes it may happen after the first year, but usually it happens after a Peahen's second year.

So, at approximately age 2 to 3, the Peahen will lay her first eggs. This happens in early spring and runs into summer.

During that time, the Peahen will lay one egg per day for around 6 to 10 days. Then she sits on them and protects her unborn children until they hatch.

It takes **28** days for the chicks to be born, and soon they appear! They are eager to learn about their new home and explore. The amazing thing about Peacocks is how well formed the new chicks are. Did you know that after just one day a new chick can walk around, eat and drink without help? Isn't that amazing?

When they are born, Peachicks may remind you of turkeys with their brown and yellow plumage.

Note: Some Peacock owners have recorded Peahens laying in the fall to early winter! This is not common, but it can happen. Just another part of nature's great diversity.

Taking a break

Growing up quickly

It doesn't take long for the mother Peahen to begin training her children. During the first few days she will cover the little ones at night with her wings and rest on the ground. But after just a few days, she decides it's time for them to join her on the branches of the trees. This is difficult at first and it can be noisy too! But this skill is needed for the protection of the family. Once they learn the new skill and settle in, the mother will open her wings and shield them during the night.

It is important to know a peachick's life is not all bed and roses. A chick can lose its life if it falls from the branches. The fall to the ground is not always the issue. Sometimes a predator may come by and snatch them away.

Older peacocks may also attack the smaller chicks. Other Peahens may also chase the little chicks away from their food. So from the start, a Peachicks life is filled with challengers. But not to worry! These little chicks are strong and tough. So their chance for a full life is pretty good.

Walking with mommy

Spectacular show

The male peafowl is very good at courtship displays. But he doesn't just do anything that comes to mind. He chooses the best place and the right time to show the female how attractive he is. When a Peahen is coming close, the male Peacock stirs into action. First, he lifts his tail into the air. Then he displays his back feathers which are not too colorful. He may move around, go back and forth and even sway from side to side.

As the Peahen gets closer, the male continues to show his dark feathers. The female may look him over and say no way! This is when the male gets really creative. He turns quickly and reveals all his beautiful colors in a dazzling display. The female may decide she likes him, or she may simply move on to someone else. Poor Peacock! Put your tail feathers down and try again.

If at first you don't succeed, try, try again!

A work of art

A Peacocks tail feathers is quite a work of art. There are approximately 200 shining feathers with unique eyespots. Yes, they molt, which means they lose their feathers! This usually happens during the month of August, but soon beautiful replacements start to grow again.

But the train is not the only part of a Peacock that is interesting to see. The male and females also have a crest on their heads. Have you noticed? There are beautiful feathers topped by a lovely blue-green fan and this design also gives the Peafowl a distinctive look!

The female of the species also has a crest but the color is different. The tips of the feathers are mostly of a greenish hue.

You know I look good!

Chapter 3

There are neat things we can learn about Peacocks. Would you like to know some of them?

-We already know the male of the species is called a Peacock. But do you know what the family of a Peacock is called? It's called a Bevy.

-What about a group of peafowls? Do you know what that's called? It's called a Party! Must be having a great time.

-If Peacocks are left alone for a long time they get depressed and very sad.

-Peacocks can be shy around people and it is a secretive bird. It does not give its affection that easily and even if you take care of it, it may not allow you to actually touch it. Of course there are exceptions to this rule.

-Peacocks have been admired for thousands of years and they have been kept in captivity for the same amount of time.

-In some cultures, Peacocks are worshipped as divine while in others they are seen as a sign of something bad.

- The Congo Peafowl has not been seen for a long time. More than likely this species is endangered. This applies to the Indian and Green Peafowl. Despite this issue, the Peafowl is listed as "Of least concern" by the IUCN. This refers to the International Union for Conservation of Nature.

- Alexander the Great is credited in some way with the introduction of Peacocks into Europe. But many people say Peacocks appeared before then, even as far back as 450 BC. Some people say it happened before then too! So you can see this bird species has a lot of history.

- A Peahen will usually lay between 3 – 5 eggs. But some may lay even more. It could be between 3 -12 eggs! This group of eggs is called a "clutch."

Part of the family

Peacocks are truly amazing birds, but is there anything else we can learn about them? What about having one as a pet? There are many people who enjoy raising this multicolored bird. But what is the best way to do it?

According to the website 'StarShine Ranch' Peafowls love certain things in a certain way. Consider the following tips:

-Peafowl like respect and to be treated with dignity. That means no chasing them around. After all, if a Peacock needs to show his best side it can't be chased around ruffling its feathers!

-They love open spaces to walk about and show their thing! This means strutting around like a…Yes! You got it…a Peacock.

-Trees are wonderful. Peafowl love trees so they can rest high and dry. And this helps them to relax because they know it is difficult for predators to reach them.

-Good neighbors are ideal. So if a Peafowl has good company all will be well in their little world.

Note: If anyone of these factors is missing in a Peacocks life, they may wander off for finer pastures!

So when you first get a Peacock they may not sit still for a little while. They may leave and wander away looking for their original "home." This means a little confinement is a great way to keep you bird safe and protected. The number of days varies, but 'Starshine Ranch' suggests no longer than a week.

Feeding them should not be too difficult as they like most things. However, protein is a necessary element to keep them healthy and strong. Two times per day is the recommended amount, but during the winter months, this could extend to three times.

And don't forget to give them treats from time to time! This could be berries, peanuts, raisins, grapes and their favorites: Black sunflower seeds.

A word of caution: These birds can be aggressive depending on their care. So if you go to a zoo area or park and see Peacocks, be careful. Why? If this bird has been mistreated in the past or hurt in any way, it may react when you least expect it. A healthy degree of caution is needed! You could also ask the park officials if it is safe to approach or feed the bird.

FUN FACTS FOR KIDS: Peacocks are very beautiful but they have an interesting voice. Many people refer to it as ugly but you may prefer to call it unique. *Wikipedia* notes the cry may sound like a loud "pia-ow or may-awe." There are other calls too like ka-aan or a quick kok-kok. They even explode with a low pitch honk when they get upset.

Conclusion

Keeping an eye on things

In conclusion:

Peacocks are fascinating birds with lovely feathers in colorful hues. They can be mysterious, make you laugh or inspire your artistic flair.

For thousands of years, this species has been a part of our lives. There are many legends about this beautiful bird and over the years more stories and and legends have been added. And even today it continues to impress us.

A Peacocks unique personality may seem intimidating at first, and it is true you need to be careful when dealing with this species. But with the right supervision and the proper respect for all animals, you can learn to appreciate this magnificent bird.

As with all of Earth's creatures, Peafowls are a great part of earth's tapestry of life. So the next time you see this bird on TV, at the zoo or at a park, stop for just a moment to admire one of nature's ancient wonders!

Author Bio

K. Bennett is a native from the Island of Roatan, North of Honduras. She loves to write about many different subjects, but writing for children is special to her heart.

Some of her favorite pastimes are reading, traveling and discovering new things. These activities help to fuel her imagination and act like a canvas for more stories.

She also loves fantasy elements like hidden worlds and faraway lands. Basically anything that gets her imagination soaring to new heights!

Her writing credits include children books online, short stories for online magazines, and two novellas listed at Amazon.com

Our books are available at

1. Amazon.com

2. Barnes and Noble

3. Itunes

4 Kobo

5. Smashwords

6. Google Play Books

This book is published by

JD-Biz Corp

P O Box 374

Mendon, Utah 84325

http://www.jd-biz.com/

Peacocks

Peacocks

Peacocks

Made in the USA
Middletown, DE
06 February 2020